HAPPY, HEALTHY, *and* FREE

Happy, Healthy, and Free: A 31-Day Wellness Journey

Copyright © 2025 Breakfast for Seven

All rights reserved. No part of this book may be reproduced or transmitted in any form or by any means, electronic or mechanical, including photocopying, recording, or by any information storage and retrieval system, without permission in writing from the publisher.

Unless otherwise noted, Scripture quotations marked TPT are taken from The Passion Translation®. Copyright © 2017, 2018, 2020 by Passion & Fire Ministries, Inc. Used by permission. All rights reserved. ThePassionTranslation.com.

Scripture quotations marked AMP are taken from the Amplified® Bible, Copyright © 1954, 1958, 1962, 1964, 1965, 1987 by The Lockman Foundation. Used by permission. lockman.org

Scripture quotations marked ESV from The ESV® Bible (The Holy Bible, English Standard Version®), © 2001 by Crossway, a publishing ministry of Good News Publishers. All rights reserved.

Scripture quotations marked KJV are taken from the King James Version®. Public domain.

Scripture quotations marked MEV are taken from The Holy Bible, Modern English Version. Copyright © 2014 by Military Bible Association. All rights reserved.

Scripture quotations marked MSG are taken from *The Message*, copyright © 1993, 2002, 2018 by Eugene H. Peterson. Used by permission of NavPress. All rights reserved. Represented by Tyndale House Publishers.

Scripture quotations marked NASB are taken from the (NASB®) New American Standard Bible®, Copyright © 1960, 1971, 1977, 1995, 2020 by The Lockman Foundation. Used by permission. All rights reserved. lockman.org

Scripture quotations marked NIV are taken from the Holy Bible, New International Version®, NIV®. Copyright © 1973, 1978, 1984, 2011 by Biblica, Inc.™ Used by permission of Zondervan. All rights reserved worldwide. http://www.zondervan.com The "NIV" and "New International Version" are trademarks registered in the United States Patent and Trademark Office by Biblica, Inc.™

Scripture quotations marked NKJV are taken from the New King James Version®. Copyright © 1982 by Thomas Nelson. Used by permission. All rights reserved.

Scripture quotations marked NLT are taken from the Holy Bible, New Living Translation, copyright © 1996, 2004, 2015 by Tyndale House Foundation. Used by permission of Tyndale House Publishers, Carol Stream, Illinois 60188. All rights reserved.

Scripture quotations marked TLB are taken from The Living Bible, copyright © 1971 by Tyndale House Foundation. Used by permission of Tyndale House Publishers, Carol Stream, Illinois 60188. All rights reserved.

ISBN: 978-1-963492-31-6

Produced by Breakfast for Seven
breakfastforseven.com

Printed in the United States of America.

HAPPY, HEALTHY, and FREE

A 31-Day Wellness Journey

CONTENTS

Introduction vi

Part 1: God's Will Is Health

01 Wholly Whole 2
02 No Sickness in the Garden 6
03 "I Am the Lord Who Heals You" 10
04 Jesus Healed Them All 14
05 Total Well-Being 18

Part 2: Health for Your Spirit

06 Once Dead, Now Alive 24
07 A Spirit-to-Spirit Conversation 28
08 Reborn to Supernatural Life 32
09 So Much Good News 36
10 Super-Alive 40

Part 3: Health for Your Soul

11 He Restores Your Soul 46
12 Healed of Shame 50
13 Healed of Fear and Anxiousness 54
14 Healing for the Brokenhearted 58
15 The Cure for a Downcast Soul 62

Part 4: Health for Your Body

16 God's Will Concerning Your Healing 68
17 Forgiven and Healed 72
18 You Were Healed 76
19 All Your Diseases 80
20 Redeemed from Destruction 84
21 Your Youth Renewed 88
22 He Sent His Word 92
23 What Good Fathers Do 96
24 Be Free From Your Suffering 100
25 Gifts of Healings 104
26 Abundant, Overflowing Zoe Life 108
27 Your Healing God 112
28 Call the Elders 116

Part 5: Wholeness at the Lord's Table

29 Healing in the Passover Meal 122
30 His Body, Broken for You 126
31 Redeemed By His Blood 130

INTRODUCTION

This 31-day devotional was prayerfully crafted to help you receive a truth that is woven throughout the New Testament: Salvation in Jesus Christ is not only about eternal life in heaven, but it is also for life here on earth.

Salvation transforms every part of our being. When you received Jesus as Lord of your life, you also received access to the benefits of becoming a son or daughter of God. Salvation means you were adopted into the family of God and now can walk boldly into the throne room of grace and mercy and receive every good gift your heavenly Father has for you.

One of those gifts is the gift of health and wholeness.

This journey is about more than just faith—it's about stepping into a life that is *happy, healthy,* and *free.* Over the next 31 days, you will embark on a wellness journey that invites you to embrace God's plan for your spirit, soul, and body. His desire is for you to thrive in every area of life—experiencing the fullness of His joy, the wholeness of His healing, and the freedom that comes through His Word.

God is better than we know. He is more grand than we can comprehend. The blessings made available to us are wonderfully glorious. You can be wholly whole. You can receive God's perfect blessing for your life and experience what it means to be *happy, healthy,* and *free.*

In the garden of Eden, there was no sickness, no fear, and no death. That was God's original design. And through Jesus, that perfect plan was restored! When Jesus went to the Cross, He bore our sin, our pain, our sickness, and our brokenness. Every wound, every burden, every chain was covered through His finished work.

As a child of the Most High God, you can receive the blessing of health and wholeness today. Consider these wonderful scriptures:

- *Now, may the God of peace and harmony set you apart, making you completely holy. And may your entire being— spirit, soul, and body—be kept completely flawless in the appearing of our Lord Jesus, the Anointed One. The one who calls you by name is trustworthy and will thoroughly complete his work in you* (1 Thessalonians 5:23–24).

- *He endured the punishment that made us completely whole, and in his wounding we found our healing* (Isaiah 53:5).

You can receive God's best for your life. You can live in His ideas, His plans, and His will. Over these next 31 days, receive the promises of God, strengthen your faith, and believe you can step into God's wonderful gift of wholeness as you walk in divine health and supernatural peace.

PART 1

GOD'S WILL IS HEALTH

HAPPY, HEALTHY, AND FREE

DAY
01

WHOLLY WHOLE

Now, may the God of peace and harmony set you apart, making you completely holy. And may your entire being—spirit, soul, and body—be kept completely flawless in the appearing of our Lord Jesus, the Anointed One. The one who calls you by name is trustworthy and will thoroughly complete his work in you.

1 THESSALONIANS 5:23–24

Here in Paul's benediction of blessing over the believers in Thessalonica we see one of the Bible's clearest indications that we are all comprised of three parts. We are *spirit, soul, and body.*

You may be more familiar with the venerable King James Version's rendering of verse 23: *And the very God of peace sanctify you **wholly*** . . . . The Greek word translated "peace" in that opening verse means to be in a state of calm, harmony, and wholeness.

The witness of Scripture is clear. You are a three-part being, and God cares passionately about all three aspects of who YOU are. The salvation Jesus paid an enormous price to provide for you encompasses not just your spirit but your soul and body as well. God's will is that you become "wholly whole."

YOUR WHOLENESS BLESSING

May you understand and embrace the truth that Jesus died to sanctify, save, restore, renew, and redeem *all* of you. May you open your heart to the reality that, in Him, you can be "wholly whole."

THE WITNESS OF
SCRIPTURE IS CLEAR.
YOU ARE A THREE-PART
BEING, AND GOD CARES
PASSIONATELY ABOUT
ALL THREE ASPECTS
OF WHO YOU ARE.

HAPPY, HEALTHY, AND FREE

DAY
02

NO SICKNESS IN THE GARDEN

God surveyed all he had made and said, "I love it!" For it pleased him greatly. Evening gave way to morning—day six.

GENESIS 1:31

You don't have to wonder about what God wants for mankind in general or for you in particular. The Bible shows us precisely what God's will is. It's right there in the very first chapter.

When God finished His work of creation, He surveyed it and pronounced it *very good* (v. 31, KJV), or, as The Passion Translation renders it, God said, *"I love it!"*

So, ask yourself this question: Was there any sickness, weakness, or brokenness in the garden when God pronounced it "good"? Of course not. The fall of man broke humanity and creation — distorting and disfiguring what God has previously declared perfect.

Yes, there are questions and mysteries surrounding healing and how it is accessed, but of one thing we can be certain: God's will for you is healing, health, and wholeness.

YOUR WHOLENESS BLESSING

May all doubt about God's will for your health be removed. May you be filled with confidence that God, through the sacrifice of His Son, opened the way for you to return to Him and to the wholeness and soundness over which He shouted, *"I love it!"*

THE BIBLE SHOWS US PRECISELY WHAT GOD'S WILL IS.

HAPPY, HEALTHY, AND FREE

DAY
03

"I AM THE LORD WHO HEALS YOU"

"... I will not make you suffer the diseases I sent on the Egyptians, for I am the Lord who heals you."

EXODUS 15:26 (TLB)

One of the most important things any believer can learn is that there are key differences between the old and new covenants. While Hebrews 8:6 says the new covenant is better than the old one and is based on better promises, one thing remains true in both: *God loves to heal.*

In Exodus, we find God essentially introducing Himself to a 12-tribe nation of people who knew virtually nothing about Him. One of the first things He lets them know is that He is a healer of His covenant people: *"I am the Lord who heals you."*

Yet that very truth has been lost to so many of His covenant people today. How tragic this is! It is a truth that presents itself over and over in the Scriptures. The God who loves you, pursued you, and sent His only begotten Son to die for you wants you to be assured of this aspect of His identity. He is *"the Lord who heals you."*

YOUR WHOLENESS BLESSING

May you come to understand in the deepest part of your being that your Father-God loves to heal. He loves it so much that He introduces Himself as a healer to those new to covenant relationship with Him.

HE IS A HEALER OF HIS COVENANT PEOPLE: *"I AM THE LORD WHO HEALS YOU."*

HAPPY, HEALTHY, AND FREE

DAY
04

JESUS HEALED THEM ALL

Jesus ministered from place to place throughout all of the province of Galilee. He taught in the synagogues, preaching the wonderful news of the kingdom and healing every kind of sickness and disease among the people. His fame spread throughout all Syria! Many people who were in pain and suffering with every kind of illness were brought to Jesus for their healing—epileptics, paralytics, and those tormented by demonic powers were all set free. Everyone who was brought to Jesus was healed!

MATTHEW 4:23–24

Jesus plainly stated that He only did the things He saw His heavenly Father doing (John 5:19). And throughout the Gospels we see Jesus healing every individual who came to Him. For example, in Matthew 12:15, we read: . . . *Massive crowds followed him from there, and* **he healed all who were sick** (emphasis added).

Furthermore, the writer of Hebrews tells us that Jesus is a living, breathing, walking, talking representation of God's nature, character, and values: *The Son is the dazzling radiance of God's splendor, the exact expression of God's true nature—his mirror image! . . .* (Hebrews 1:3).

Oh, what encouraging news this is. When we're facing sickness, weakness, or brokenness in body, soul, or spirit, we don't have to wonder and speculate about the position of the Father or the Son. Settling this question is the vital first step in appropriating the wholeness Jesus died to make possible for you.

YOUR WHOLENESS BLESSING

Whenever you are tempted to doubt God's will for your wholeness, may you remember that Jesus never once refused a person who came to Him for healing, deliverance, or restoration. Not once. He was and is the perfect representation of the Father's values and will.

JESUS IS A LIVING, BREATHING, WALKING, TALKING REPRESENTATION OF GOD'S NATURE, CHARACTER, AND VALUES.

HAPPY, HEALTHY, AND FREE

DAY
05

TOTAL WELL-BEING

. . . He endured the punishment that made us completely whole, and in his wounding we found our healing.

ISAIAH 53:5

If the wording of today's key verse seems unfamiliar to you, perhaps you are more acquainted with the King James rendering of that verse, . . . *the chastisement of our peace was upon him; and with his stripes we are healed.*

The Hebrew word translated "peace" in the KJV is *shalom*. It does indeed mean "peace," but that English word brings us only a sliver of its original meaning. The Passion Translation's choice of *completely whole* is much closer to the true meaning of *shalom*.

When an ancient Israelite spoke the word *shalom* as a blessing or greeting, he or she was wishing for your total well-being — a state of wholeness and completeness wherein nothing is missing or broken.

Now apply this new understanding to the insight the prophet Isaiah gave us about the suffering and sacrificial death of Jesus. The wounds — the breaking and destruction of His body — made the way for you to be completely whole.

YOUR WHOLENESS BLESSING

May you embrace and appropriate to the fullest the truth that Jesus was broken to make you fully whole — complete, equipped, and provisioned in every way, with nothing missing or broken.

WHEN AN ANCIENT ISRAELITE SPOKE THE WORD *SHALOM* AS A BLESSING OR GREETING, HE OR SHE WAS WISHING FOR YOUR TOTAL WELL-BEING.

PART 2

HEALTH FOR YOUR SPIRIT

HAPPY, HEALTHY, AND FREE

DAY
06

ONCE DEAD, NOW ALIVE

And his fullness fills you, even though you were once like corpses, dead in your sins and offenses.

EPHESIANS 2:1

In the opening chapters of Genesis, we see God warning Adam and Eve to avoid the fruit of the Tree of Knowledge of Good and Evil. He said that *"on the day that you eat from it you will certainly die"* (Genesis 2:17, NASB). Not you'll die "someday," not "eventually" — no, God said they would die on the very day they ate from it. Yet they didn't, did they? Or *did* they?

They didn't die physically that day, but they did die spiritually. Indeed, in today's key verse, Paul tells us that every Christian was formerly *dead in your sins*. But the good news is that changes the instant you are born again. As Paul makes clear four verses later, *But because of his great love for us, God . . . made us alive with Christ . . .* (Ephesians 2:4–5, NIV).

The spiritual deadness passed down to every descendant of Adam and Eve is reversed the moment you say "yes" to God's extraordinary offer of eternal life in Jesus. Is there any greater form of healing than being made fully and forever alive with Christ?

YOUR WHOLENESS BLESSING

May you recognize that your former deadness of spirit has been healed by the One who conquered death and offers abundant life. May you recognize that *His fullness fills you*.

THE SPIRITUAL DEADNESS PASSED DOWN TO EVERY DESCENDANT OF ADAM AND EVE IS REVERSED THE MOMENT YOU SAY "YES" TO GOD'S EXTRAORDINARY OFFER OF ETERNAL LIFE IN JESUS.

DAY 07

A SPIRIT-TO-SPIRIT CONVERSATION

And you did not receive the "spirit of religious duty," leading you back into the fear of never being good enough. But you have received the "Spirit of full acceptance," enfolding you into the family of God. And you will never feel orphaned, for as he rises up within us, our spirits join him in saying the words of tender affection, "Beloved Father!" For the Holy Spirit makes God's fatherhood real to us as he whispers into our innermost being, "You are God's beloved child!"

ROMANS 8:15–16

Notice how frequently the word *spirit* appears in today's key verses. Also note that the term *innermost being* in the final sentence carries the same meaning as *spirit*. You were created a three-part being — spirit, soul, and body. And at the level of our spirits, the fall of mankind left us all destitute orphans.

Yet many believers don't really understand the many miraculous, wonderful things that happen on a spiritual level the instant they are born again. Those miracles include not just the act of being adopted by a loving heavenly Father but also receiving an inner spiritual "knowing" that we have indeed been fully accepted, received, and incorporated into God's family.

Listen with the ears of your spirit. Attune your innermost being to that whisper. You'll hear the best news any former orphan can receive: *"You are God's beloved child!"*

YOUR WHOLENESS BLESSING

May you clearly hear the Holy Spirit of God whispering the news that you belong to the Father. May you absorb into your identity the truth that the One who made you spiritually alive and healed your orphan spirit now testifies that you have been accepted into God's family.

MANY BELIEVERS DON'T REALLY UNDERSTAND THE MANY MIRACULOUS, WONDERFUL THINGS THAT HAPPEN ON A SPIRITUAL LEVEL THE INSTANT THEY ARE BORN AGAIN.

HAPPY, HEALTHY, AND FREE

DAY 08

REBORN TO SUPERNATURAL LIFE

Jesus answered, "I speak an eternal truth: Unless you are born of water and the Spirit, you will never enter God's kingdom. For the natural realm only gives birth to things that are natural, but the spiritual realm gives birth to supernatural life!"

JOHN 3:5–6

In Jesus' remarkable conversation with Nicodemus in John 3, He reveals an extraordinary truth. In fact, if John hadn't delivered these words of Jesus to us in his Gospel, our understanding of "the new birth" would be far thinner and poorer.

Here, right from the Savior's lips, we learn that Christians experience two births. In this passage, "born of water" refers to an expectant mother's water breaking and a baby being born, which is how we all enter the world. But Jesus also goes on to speak of a second, spiritual birth.

Those who experience this second birth have literally moved from spiritual death to *supernatural life!* Ephesians 2:5 puts it this way: *Even when we were dead and doomed in our many sins, he united us into the very life of Christ and saved us by his wonderful grace!*

The moment you said "yes" to Jesus, your spirit became fully alive with supernatural life.

YOUR WHOLENESS BLESSING

May your eyes be opened to the reality that your spirit has been connected to the very life of Christ and that His life now empowers and illuminates you.

THE MOMENT YOU SAID "YES" TO JESUS, YOUR SPIRIT BECAME FULLY ALIVE WITH SUPERNATURAL LIFE.

HAPPY, HEALTHY, AND FREE

DAY
09

SO MUCH GOOD NEWS

Now Christ lives his life in you! And even though your body may be dead because of the effects of sin, his life-giving Spirit imparts life to you because you are fully accepted by God. Yes, God raised Jesus to life! And since God's Spirit of Resurrection lives in you, he will also raise your dying body to life by the same Spirit that breathes life into you!

ROMANS 8:10–11

Many passages in the Scriptures contain at least one mind-blowing concept. Some contain two. But it would be difficult to find two consecutive verses in the Bible that hold more good-news bombshells than in today's key verses.

Here, in the heart of one of the richest chapters in the entire Bible, we find the following revelations:

1. Jesus is living His life in you and through you.

2. Although we all will die one day, the *life-giving* Holy Spirit continually *imparts life to you.*

3. Why? Because *you are fully accepted by God!*

Yet, as the pitchmen on TV commercials say, "But wait! There's more!"

4. The very same Spirit that brought Jesus out of the grip of death is now living and working within you, not only guaranteeing your own resurrection in the future but also continually imparting life to you *now*.

That's a lot of good news in two verses. Receive and believe by faith all of these truths today.

YOUR WHOLENESS BLESSING

May you be filled with the comforting, confidence-building knowledge that, because you are fully accepted by God, your spirit is continually receiving life from the same Spirit of resurrection that raised Jesus from the dead.

JESUS IS LIVING HIS LIFE IN YOU AND THROUGH YOU.

HAPPY, HEALTHY, AND FREE

DAY
10

SUPER-ALIVE

Even when we were dead and doomed in our many sins, he united us into the very life of Christ and saved us by his wonderful grace! He raised us up with Christ the exalted One, and we ascended with him into the glorious perfection and authority of the heavenly realm, for we are now co-seated as one with Christ!

EPHESIANS 2:5–6

*R*egeneration. That's the fancy word theologians use to describe the reality that believers were once spiritually dead but are now very much alive. More than alive, really. At the level of your spirit, you are super-alive because you're spiritually connected to and merged with the very Source of life.

This is a mind-blowing thing to contemplate, yet the Bible makes it very clear that this is the case. We also see it in 2 Peter 1:3–4:

> *Everything we could ever need for life and godliness* ***has already been deposited in us*** *by his divine power. . . . As a result of this, he has given you magnificent promises that are beyond all price, so that through the power of these tremendous promises* ***we can experience partnership with the divine nature****, by which you have escaped the corrupt desires that are of the world* (emphasis added).

Being "born-again" is far, far more than just a ticket to heaven when you die. At the level of your spirit, you are super-alive now in this life.

YOUR WHOLENESS BLESSING

May you live this day in full recognition that the very life of Christ has not only saved you, but He has also filled you, at the level of your spirit, with His divine power.

BEING "BORN-AGAIN" IS FAR, FAR MORE THAN JUST A TICKET TO HEAVEN WHEN YOU DIE.

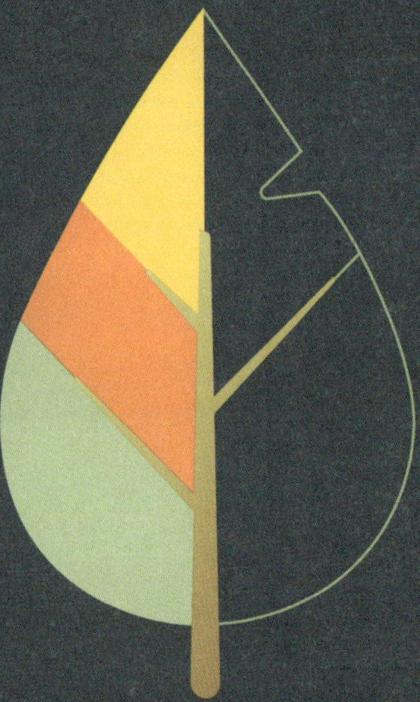

PART 3

HEALTH FOR YOUR SOUL

HAPPY, HEALTHY, AND FREE

DAY 11

HE RESTORES YOUR SOUL

[The Lord, my Shepherd] offers a resting place for me in his luxurious love. His tracks take me to an oasis of peace near the quiet brook of bliss. That's where he restores and revives my life . . . .

PSALM 23:2–3

Throughout this 31-day devotional, we're focusing on receiving supernatural healing and wholeness in all three parts of your being — spirit, soul, and body. But what, exactly, is the soul?

The widely accepted definition of the word *soul* is "one's mind, will, and emotions." In other words, your soul is where you *think, choose,* and *feel.*

Today's key verses are The Passion Translation's take on these familiar lines from the 23rd Psalm: *He makes me to lie down in green pastures; He leads me beside the still waters. He restores my soul . . .* (NKJV).

Living in this fallen world filled with broken people tends to take a toll on our souls. Stress, anxiety, worry, disappointment, frustration, anger . . . these and a hundred other realities of life can make us "soul sick." And chronic sickness of the soul often leads to sickness in our bodies.

That's why it's the best possible news to hear that you belong to a Shepherd who, if you will let Him, wants to guide you to a place where your soul can be restored and healed — to *an oasis of peace near the quiet brook of bliss.*

YOUR WHOLENESS BLESSING

May you let the Good Shepherd guide you daily to His blissful place of rest, refreshment, and healing for your soul.

YOUR SOUL IS WHERE YOU *THINK, CHOOSE*, AND *FEEL.*

HAPPY, HEALTHY, AND FREE

DAY
12

HEALED OF SHAME

Looking unto Jesus, the author and finisher of our faith, who for the joy that was set before Him endured the cross, despising the shame, and has sat down at the right hand of the throne of God.

HEBREWS 12:2 (NKJV)

Shame was the first visible evidence that Adam and Eve had fallen and had unleashed something terrible upon themselves and upon the whole world. Prior to that fateful day, they happily stood before God naked yet unashamed. Another way to describe their original state is "un-*self*-conscious." After that day, shame, produced by guilt, permeated their souls and the soul of every one of their descendants.

This explains why shame is such a central feature of all Jesus suffered on the day He died for us. Every moment of the crucifixion narrative was intensely shameful and shaming. It began with a very public mocking, beating, and spitting. It ended with the sinless Savior of the world hanging naked from the Cross within view of people entering or leaving the city of Jerusalem.

Why naked? Because Jesus was bearing the shame of all mankind. And because Adam and Eve's awareness of their nakedness was the initial sign that something had severed their life-sustaining connection to God. Jesus bore your shame so your soul could be saved and made whole in every way.

YOUR WHOLENESS BLESSING

May you refuse to carry anything Jesus bore on the Cross for you. And that includes any sense of shame concerning what you've done or what has been done to you.

JESUS BORE YOUR
SHAME SO YOUR SOUL
COULD BE SAVED
AND MADE WHOLE
IN EVERY WAY.

HAPPY, HEALTHY, AND FREE

DAY
13

HEALED OF FEAR AND ANXIOUSNESS

*Perfect, absolute peace surrounds those whose imaginations are consumed with you; they confidently trust in you. Yes, trust in the Lord Y*AHWEH *forever and ever . . . !*

ISAIAH 26:3–4

The human imagination is a powerful gift from God. It's alive and active when you read a book or hear a great story told. It paints vivid pictures on the canvas of your mind and plays out technicolor movies on the inner screen of your soul.

Your imagination enables you to experience things that you have never actually experienced. And, for better or worse, it enables you to visualize a possible future that has not yet happened.

The "worse" part comes when the enemy of our souls tricks us into turning that ability around and using it as a weapon against ourselves. He will give you lots of encouragement to vividly imagine a dark future filled with negative outcomes. And neurologists tell us that when you are actively imagining that dark future, your nervous system and body respond as if those terrible things are *really* happening to you, which is why chronic fear and anxiety can literally make you sick.

The solution is to use your God-given imagination for its intended purpose — to visualize the good things Jesus made available to you through His sacrifice. (That's called "hope.") And to simply put your confidence and trust in Him.

YOUR WHOLENESS BLESSING

May your imagination be consumed with God and His goodness as you are surrounded by perfect peace.

USE YOUR GOD-GIVEN IMAGINATION FOR ITS INTENDED PURPOSE — TO VISUALIZE THE GOOD THINGS JESUS MADE AVAILABLE TO YOU THROUGH HIS SACRIFICE.

HAPPY, HEALTHY, AND FREE

DAY
14

HEALING FOR THE BROKENHEARTED

The Lord is near to the brokenhearted and saves the crushed in spirit.

PSALM 34:18 (ESV)

"Where were You, God?" That's a very human, very understandable question many believers ask when the worst imaginable thing happens. Many believers lay the blame for their crushing disappointments at the feet of their loving heavenly Father because they wrongly believe God is responsible.

When he was a boy, media mogul Ted Turner considered being a missionary. Then, as a young man, he watched his younger sister die a terrible death at age 17 from a rare form of lupus. A few years later, Ted's father committed suicide. These heartbreaking events caused Ted to blame God and profess to be an atheist for much of his adult life. In his latter years, he softened his hostility toward God, but he spent decades of his life tormented by the belief that God was behind the death of people He loved.

Taken as a whole, the witness of Scripture is in harmony with today's key verse. The world is filled with pain and brokenness because of the fall of mankind and the curse that it unleashed upon the earth, but God is *not* the cause of suffering. He's the answer to it. In fact, He moved heaven and earth to send His only Son to the earth as one of us so the curse could be reversed in our lives.

Where was God when your heart was broken? He was near. He still is — ready to comfort, heal, and restore.

YOUR WHOLENESS BLESSING

May you sense God's nearness and compassion in your darkest moments. May you receive the healing of your soul that only He can bring.

GOD IS *NOT* THE CAUSE OF SUFFERING. HE'S THE ANSWER TO IT.

HAPPY, HEALTHY, AND FREE

DAY
15

THE CURE FOR A DOWNCAST SOUL

Bless the Lord, O my soul; and all that is within me, bless His holy name!

PSALM 103:1 (NIV)

David talked to his own soul. We see this in a number of his psalms, including the one that contains today's key verse. He knew something we need to know: sometimes our souls just need a good pep talk. Sometimes your mind, will, and emotions need to be reminded of some biblical truths.

In another psalm we find: *Why are you in despair, O my soul? And why are you restless and disturbed within me? Hope in God and wait expectantly for Him . . .* (Psalm 43:5, AMP).

When this psalmist recognized that his soul was downcast and in despair; when he realized he was starting to wallow in self-pity; he knew the prescription that would bring the cure. That prescription is hope. He was saying, "Hey soul, put your hope in God!"

Hope is a powerful thing. It's the natural byproduct of recognizing that God is good, He loves us, and He causes all things to work together for our good (Romans 8:28). When you remind yourself of those three truths, it's easier to shift your soul into a better state.

Feelings can deceive us. It's vital to remember that there is a higher level of truth than emotions. That higher truth is who God is and what He has done for us through Jesus.

YOUR WHOLENESS BLESSING

When your soul is downcast, may you remind yourself of all of the benefits of being His beloved child; and may you direct your soul toward hope in Him.

FEELINGS CAN DECEIVE US. IT'S VITAL TO REMEMBER THAT THERE IS A HIGHER LEVEL OF TRUTH THAN EMOTIONS.

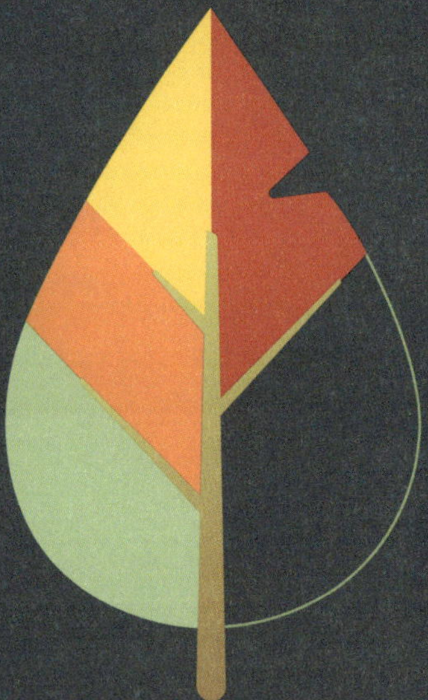

PART 4

HEALTH FOR YOUR BODY

HAPPY, HEALTHY, AND FREE

DAY
16

GOD'S WILL CONCERNING *YOUR* HEALING

Jesus traveled throughout the region of Galilee, teaching in the synagogues and announcing the Good News about the Kingdom. And he healed every kind of disease and illness. News about him spread as far as Syria, and people soon began bringing to him all who were sick. And whatever their sickness or disease, or if they were demon possessed or epileptic or paralyzed—he healed them all.

MATTHEW 4:23–24 (NLT)

Most Christians believe God *can* heal. (*Of course he can. He's God!*) Many believe God *does* occasionally heal someone miraculously. But a vast majority of believers, when they personally are sick or injured, are unsure as to whether or not it is God's will to heal *them*. This uncertainty means they pray for healing with very little faith, hope, or expectancy. (And praying with low faith, hope, and expectancy isn't exactly a prescription for seeing miracles.)

The Bible is very clear: Jesus is a perfect and accurate representation of God's character, values, and ways. Hebrews 1:3 tells us Jesus is *the exact representation of His nature* (NASB). Paul tells us, *Christ is the visible image of the invisible God* (Colossians 1:15, NLT). And Jesus Himself said, "*. . . the Son can do nothing by himself; he can do only what he sees his Father doing, because whatever the Father does the Son also does*" (John 5:19, NIV).

Keep that truth in mind as you read the Gospels. Jesus made every person who came to Him whole. He broke up every funeral He encountered by raising the dead to life. No blind, deaf, or diseased person ever came to Jesus for help and went away disappointed.

What is God's will for *your* healing? You'll find your answer in four words: Jesus healed them all.

YOUR WHOLENESS BLESSING

May you be filled with faith, hope, and expectancy when you come to Jesus with a need for healing.

JESUS IS A PERFECT AND ACCURATE REPRESENTATION OF GOD'S CHARACTER, VALUES, AND WAYS.

HAPPY, HEALTHY, AND FREE

DAY
17

FORGIVEN *AND* HEALED

"Which is easier to say, 'Your sins are forgiven,' or, 'Stand up and walk!'? But now, to convince you that the Son of Man has been given authority to forgive sins, I say to this man, 'Stand up, pick up your mat, and walk home.'" Immediately the man sprang to his feet and left for home.

MATTHEW 9:5–7

Jesus' words, quoted in today's key verses, come near the end of the account of the paraplegic man who was lowered down through a hole in the roof of a house where Jesus was speaking. One remarkable aspect of that story is how Jesus merged the subjects of healing and forgiveness of sin.

Why? Because sickness entered the world because of sin. Had Adam and Eve not rebelled, sickness would not have plagued humanity. Jesus' mission was to not only deal with sin but the results of sin — including sickness. A reading of Isaiah's prophecy that foresees Jesus' atoning death on the Cross makes this crystal clear:

> *Yet he was the one who carried our sicknesses and endured the torment of our sufferings. . . . But it was because of our rebellious deeds that he was pierced and because of our sins that he was crushed. He endured the punishment that made us completely whole, and in his wounding we found our healing* (Isaiah 53:4–5).

Read that entire passage and you'll see Isaiah prophetically looking forward to the Cross and seeing Jesus not only dealing with our sins but with the effects of our sins, including oppression, sorrow, grief, and, yes, sickness.

YOUR WHOLENESS BLESSING

If you have faith that, because of Jesus, your sins are forgiven, may you also have equal faith that in *his wounding*, [you] *have* [your] *healing*.

JESUS' MISSION WAS TO NOT ONLY DEAL WITH SIN BUT THE RESULTS OF SIN — INCLUDING SICKNESS.

HAPPY, HEALTHY, AND FREE

DAY
18

YOU *WERE* HEALED

And He Himself brought our sins in His body up on the cross, so that we might die to sin and live for righteousness; by His wounds you were healed.

1 PETER 2:24 (NASB)

In yesterday's devotion, you saw the Isaiah 53 prophecy of Jesus which so vividly painted the picture of what Jesus would actually suffer roughly 500 years later. In most familiar translations, that prophecy contains the line, ". . . and by His wounds [or stripes] we are healed." The verb in that phrase ("are") is always rendered in the present tense.

So, it should cause us to lean forward and take note when the apostle Peter changes the verb to past tense in 1 Peter 2:24. There, quoting Isaiah, he writes: *by His wounds you **were** healed* (emphasis added). Isaiah wrote centuries before the Cross. Peter was writing several decades after the Cross. The implication is that Jesus didn't just make it possible for you to possibly be healed someday. But rather, His atoning death already made full provision for your healing.

Healing is not something you hope God *will* do. It is something He's already provided through Jesus' wounds on the Cross. What remains is not, somehow, persuading a reluctant God. As with salvation, it is a matter of receiving.

YOUR WHOLENESS BLESSING

May you have grace to have wide-open arms to receive everything Jesus purchased for you through His suffering, death, and resurrection — including supernatural healing.

JESUS DIDN'T JUST MAKE IT POSSIBLE FOR YOU TO POSSIBLY BE HEALED SOMEDAY. BUT RATHER, HIS ATONING DEATH ALREADY MADE FULL PROVISION FOR YOUR HEALING.

HAPPY, HEALTHY, AND FREE

DAY
19

ALL YOUR DISEASES

Bless the Lord, O my soul, and forget not all His benefits: Who forgives all your iniquities, Who heals all your diseases.

PSALM 103:2–3 (NKJV)

In a previous devotion, we looked at Psalm 103:1 as evidence that David would speak to his soul. The two verses that follow that verse hold more important truth for us. It's easy for most of us to believe that, through Jesus' sacrifice, God has forgiven us. But that is only one of the "benefits" of salvation. As David reminds us here, another is healing.

Note the word *all* in verse 3. *All* is a wonderful word, isn't it? Not some. Not a few. *All*. This is one of scores of verses that reveal the reality that provision for physical healing was part of Jesus' atoning work on the Cross — in addition to provision for washing away our sins.

The Hebrew word translated "diseases" in that verse is the plural form of the word *tachalu*. It's a word that, according to *Strong's Concordance*, means "great pain, horrible torment, i.e., to have a high degree of physical pain and discomfort."

Jesus bore all of that for us on the Cross. Isn't that good news?

YOUR WHOLENESS BLESSING

May you have as much faith to receive healing as you have faith to receive forgiveness of your sins.

PROVISION FOR PHYSICAL HEALING WAS PART OF JESUS' ATONING WORK ON THE CROSS.

HAPPY, HEALTHY, AND FREE

DAY
20

REDEEMED FROM DESTRUCTION

Bless the Lord, O my soul . . . Who redeems your life from destruction, Who crowns you with lovingkindness and tender mercies.

PSALM 103:2,4 (NKJV)

Let's continue our journey through the opening verses of the 103rd psalm. In the previous devotion, we saw that among the benefits of salvation, in addition to forgiveness of sins, is healing for all of our diseases.

In the verse that follows, we find another benefit — redemption from destruction. The Bible has a lot to say about destruction and the "Destroyer." For example, speaking of the Passover event in Exodus, Hebrews 11:28 (ESV) says, *By faith he kept the Passover and sprinkled the blood, so that the Destroyer of the firstborn might not touch them.* No rational person wants any part of either the Destroyer or destruction.

In a fallen, broken world in which countless things can destroy you, Jesus, the Redeemer, has redeemed you from destruction. That's good news! Just as the blood of an unblemished lamb painted on the doorposts of an Israelite household "redeemed" them from destruction, so the blood of Jesus *redeems your life from destruction.*

Why? Because that Redeemer was sent by an infinitely good heavenly Father whose delight is to [crown] *you with lovingkindness and tender mercies.*

YOUR WHOLENESS BLESSING

May you rest and *bless the Lord* in the knowledge that Jesus is a Redeemer whose guiltless blood has redeemed you from destruction and crowned you with kindness and mercy.

JUST AS THE BLOOD OF AN UNBLEMISHED LAMB PAINTED ON THE DOORPOSTS OF AN ISRAELITE HOUSEHOLD "REDEEMED" THEM FROM DESTRUCTION, SO THE BLOOD OF JESUS *REDEEMS YOUR LIFE FROM DESTRUCTION.*

HAPPY, HEALTHY, AND FREE

DAY
21

YOUR YOUTH RENEWED

Bless the Lord, O my soul . . . Who satisfies your mouth with good things, so that your youth is renewed like the eagle's.

PSALM 103:2,5 (NKJV)

Before we leave the opening verses of the 103rd psalm, let's make one more stop. David has been listing the benefits of being in covenant with a God who is as kind and good as our heavenly Father.

We live in a youth-obsessed culture. Untold billions of dollars are spent each year on efforts to *look* younger. The promise in Psalm 103:5 isn't primarily about how we look (although that might be a part of it), but rather about how we *feel*. A benefit of our connection to God is being strong, vigorous, pain-free, and, therefore, able to fully play our part in carrying out God's good plans and purposes for our lives.

In the book of Joshua, we find Caleb who has been forced to wait 45 years to enter the Promised Land and to slay the giants on the land God has promised to give him. Note his words:

> "... *Now, here I am this day, eighty-five years old. I am still just as strong today as I was on the day that Moses sent me. My strength now is just like my strength then, both for battle and for going out and returning*" (Joshua 14:10–11, MEV).

That's a man whose youth has been renewed like the eagle's. Why would we not embrace the same for ourselves?

YOUR WHOLENESS BLESSING

May your mouth be satisfied with good things from the Lord so that your youth is renewed. May you be strong, vigorous, and free from pain all your days.

A BENEFIT OF OUR
CONNECTION
TO GOD IS BEING
STRONG, VIGOROUS,
AND PAIN-FREE.

HAPPY, HEALTHY, AND FREE

DAY
22

HE SENT HIS WORD

He sent His word and healed them and delivered them from their destruction.

PSALM 107:20 (MEV)

Hopefully it's becoming clear to you now that God loves people and doesn't want them to be destroyed — and even clearer that your Father in heaven loves you and wants you to be well. But this presents a question: How does healing come?

The Bible's answer lies in our key verse. He sends His Word. A mountain of scriptures testify that God loves to heal and restore. Healing comes when we receive the Word on healing that He has already sent us!

God has sent that "Word." But have you received it? Put another way, has the written Word become the "living Word" to *you*?

Do you recall Jesus' encounter with the messenger of the Roman centurion who had a beloved servant who was ill? The centurion said it wasn't necessary for Jesus to come to his house in order for the servant to be healed. *The centurion replied, "Lord, I do not deserve to have you come under my roof. But just say the word, and my servant will be healed"* (Matthew 8:8, NIV).

God's Word concerning your healing will do you far more good if you'll not only read it but also receive it and speak it as the indisputable truth. Here's wonderful news: God has already sent His "Word" concerning your healing — Jesus.

YOUR WHOLENESS BLESSING

May your heart embrace the truth that God has already sent His healing Word to you and about you. His name is Jesus.

HAS THE WRITTEN WORD BECOME THE "LIVING WORD" TO *YOU*?

HAPPY, HEALTHY, AND FREE

DAY
23

WHAT GOOD FATHERS DO

"Do you know of any parent who would give his hungry child, who asked for food, a plate of rocks instead? Or when asked for a piece of fish, what parent would offer his child a snake instead? If you, imperfect as you are, know how to lovingly take care of your children and give them what's best, how much more ready is your heavenly Father to give wonderful gifts to those who ask him?"

MATTHEW 7:9–11

The world has no shortage of bad fathers. Our news feeds put some of them on display on a daily basis. But that is why they call it "news." Neglectful or abusive fathers, while more common than we wish they were, still lie outside what we consider to be normal. In all times and in all places, the vast majority of fathers feel compelled by love and duty to provide for needs of their children.

Jesus had this truth in mind when He delivered the amazing news we see in today's scripture. If flawed fathers living in this fallen, broken world provide for their children, how much more would our flawless heavenly Father provide for us?

Health and strength are two of the most basic human needs. It explains why multitudes mobbed Jesus during His ministry. And it's why health products and healthcare represent a multibillion dollar industry in the United States.

But the reality is not that God is willing to dispense healing power to you, His beloved child, should the need arise. No, God has already provided for your healing — in advance — through Jesus' suffering and sacrifice.

Of course, God has already graciously, joyously, and abundantly said "yes" to your need for healing. Why? Because He's a good Father. And that's what good fathers do.

YOUR WHOLENESS BLESSING

May you recognize that God is both good and your Father . . . making him *your* good Father.

GOD HAS ALREADY PROVIDED FOR YOUR HEALING — IN ADVANCE — THROUGH JESUS' SUFFERING AND SACRIFICE.

HAPPY, HEALTHY, AND FREE

DAY
24

BE FREE FROM YOUR SUFFERING

When the woman who experienced this miracle realized what had happened to her, she came before him, trembling with fear, and threw herself down at his feet, saying, "I was the one who touched you." And she told him her story of what had just happened. Then Jesus said to her, "Daughter, because you dared to believe, your faith has healed you. Go with peace in your heart, and be free from your suffering!"

MARK 5:33–34

You almost certainly know the story that precedes these two verses. A woman who had hemorrhaged constantly for twelve years — making her a hostage in her home and bankrupting her family — violated strict Jewish legal restrictions in one, last desperate push to get relief.

What had fueled this woman's hope? News. Reports. Testimonies about how Jesus had healed countless other people of hundreds of other incurable ailments.

She had likely heard about blind eyes being opened, withered, useless hands being restored, and previously paralyzed people running and leaping for joy. But perhaps the reports that most electrified the soul of this "untouchable" woman were those of how Jesus had healed lepers. Like women in her situation, those with leprosy could not walk freely among the people of Israel. They could not visit with friends at the market or attend weddings and hug family members they hadn't seen for years.

Believing that Jesus was both willing and able to heal her propelled this woman to press through to His Presence and Person. Nothing has changed. His Presence and Person still hold the power to make you whole. Just a touch, and you can hear Him say, *"Be free from your suffering!"*

YOUR WHOLENESS BLESSING

May the same revelation that caused that desperate woman to press into Jesus move you this very moment to press through whatever obstacles and barriers that keep you from His healing Presence.

HIS PRESENCE
AND PERSON STILL
HOLD THE POWER TO
MAKE YOU WHOLE.

HAPPY, HEALTHY, AND FREE

DAY
25

GIFTS OF HEALINGS

Jesus gathered his twelve disciples and imparted to them authority to cast out demons and to heal every sickness and every disease.

MATTHEW 10:1

Very few born-again Christians doubt the truth of today's key verse. That's because it's easy to believe that Jesus, while walking and ministering on the earth, personally healing people everywhere He went, could also delegate that healing power to His twelve handpicked disciples.

What many have difficulty accepting is that Jesus has delegated that same power to disciples like us, here and now. Many struggle to accept what Mark's Gospel says were Jesus' parting words to His disciples before being taken up into heaven: *"And these miracle signs will accompany those who believe . . . they will lay hands on the sick and heal them"* (Mark 16:17–18).

We see more evidence of this in 1 Corinthians 12 where Paul is teaching us about spiritual gifts. In that chapter, Paul mentions "gifts of healing" three times as he describes the various gifts the Holy Spirit distributes to believers. In the original Greek, that phrase is double plural and therefore is literally translated "gifts of healings."

This all makes sense when you understand this powerful truth: Jesus is *still* physically present on earth through His Body, which is made up of regular born-again believers. And through His Body, Jesus is still delivering "gifts of healings."

YOUR WHOLENESS BLESSING

May you embrace and experience the reality that Jesus still distributes gifts of healings and that He wants to give such gifts to you and deliver them through you.

JESUS IS *STILL* PHYSICALLY PRESENT ON EARTH THROUGH HIS BODY, WHICH IS MADE UP OF REGULAR BORN-AGAIN BELIEVERS.

HAPPY, HEALTHY, AND FREE

DAY
26

ABUNDANT, OVERFLOWING ZOE LIFE

"The thief comes only in order to steal and kill and destroy. I came that they may have life and enjoy life, and have it in abundance [to the full, till it overflows]."

JOHN 10:10 (AMP)

Here Jesus is drawing a stark contrast between Himself and Satan. He reveals the devil's three-fold mission: to steal, kill, and destroy. From this we can accurately derive the source of any disease or condition that seeks to "kill" you or "destroy" your health or quality of life.

Jesus then lays His own mission down beside that of the "thief" so we can see the difference. Whereas the devil comes to kill, Jesus comes to give life, and not just in small doses. No, He has come to provide it in abundant, overflowing measure.

The Greek word Jesus used that is translated "life" is an important one — *zoe*. It's a word that appears frequently in the New Testament, and it's often defined as "the God-kind of life." The leading biblical Greek dictionaries use phrases like "possessing vitality" and "absolute fullness of life" and say that the word applies to both the spiritual and physical aspects of what it means to be a human being.

Because of the way Jesus described this contrast, we can confidently say that the *zoe* life Jesus provides to us is the opposite of stealing, killing, and destroying. The thief may have come to try to steal your health, kill your body, and destroy your joy in living. But here's wonderful news: Jesus came to give you life in abundance.

YOUR WHOLENESS BLESSING

May you fully receive the *zoe* life of God into both the spiritual and physical parts of your existence — abundantly and in overflowing measure.

HERE'S WONDERFUL NEWS: JESUS CAME TO GIVE YOU LIFE IN ABUNDANCE.

HAPPY, HEALTHY, AND FREE

DAY
27

YOUR HEALING GOD

O Lord, my healing God, I cried out for a miracle and you healed me! You brought me back from the brink of death, from the depths below. Now here I am, alive and well, fully restored!

PSALM 30:2–3

There is no condition so grave that God cannot heal it. There is no diagnosis or prognosis so grim that it cannot be reversed by the Creator of the universe. There is no illness or disease so severe that it is beyond the reach of God's healing touch. Nothing . . . *nothing is impossible with God* (Luke 1:37).

Countless believers carry the testimony of having been at death's door and who today are, in the words of the psalmist, *alive and well, fully restored!* These miracles happen in a wide variety of ways. There is no one pathway of restoration. The psalmist David seems to have had this truth in mind when he wrote:

> *God is to us a God of salvation; and to God the Lord belong* **ways of escape from death** (Psalm 68:20, NASB, emphasis added).

Notice the plural in that verse: ***ways** of escape*. Numerous other translations use the phrase *escapes from death*. God is infinitely creative. So, don't look for a formula. Don't expect it to happen for you the same way it happened for someone else. But expect! He is your *healing* God.

YOUR WHOLENESS BLESSING

No matter what the diagnosis or prognosis, may you ultimately find yourself *alive and well, fully restored.*

DON'T EXPECT IT
TO HAPPEN FOR YOU
THE SAME WAY
IT HAPPENED FOR
SOMEONE ELSE.
BUT EXPECT!

HAPPY, HEALTHY, AND FREE

DAY 28

CALL THE ELDERS

Are there any sick among you? Then ask the elders of the church to come and pray over the sick and anoint them with oil in the name of our Lord. And the prayer of faith will heal the sick and the Lord will raise them up, and if they have committed sins they will be forgiven.

JAMES 5:14–15

In our ultra-individualistic culture, it's easy to forget that we are not called to live the Christian life alone. Yes, God sees us as individuals, loves us as individuals, and saves us as individuals — but He calls us to live in *community*. Faith is powerful and vital, but often we need our private faith to be joined and bolstered by the faith of others. Today's key verse is a wonderful promise that reveals two things.

First, it is yet another witness in Scripture testifying that God's desire for you is health and wholeness. We've seen testimony of this in the Old Testament, in the words and actions of Jesus, and in the events of the book of Acts. Now we have James singing the same song. Supernatural healing is available to God's people.

Second, it shows that a path — not the *only* path — but *a* path to healing is to have the faith-filled leaders of your local church community pray for you. There is power in agreement. And we can lean upon the faith of others when our faith is weak. All it requires is that we humble ourselves enough to profess that we need help.

Yes, this instruction from the apostle James contains wonderful news. In the fight against weakness, sickness, and brokenness, we do not have to fight alone.

YOUR WHOLENESS BLESSING

May you, by grace, receive the wisdom to know you do not have to fight alone and the humility to allow others to fight with you and for you.

GOD SEES US AS INDIVIDUALS, LOVES US AS INDIVIDUALS, AND SAVES US AS INDIVIDUALS — BUT HE CALLS US TO LIVE IN *COMMUNITY*.

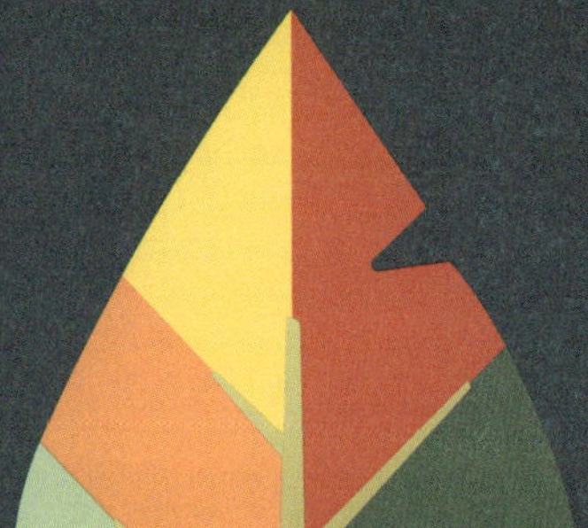

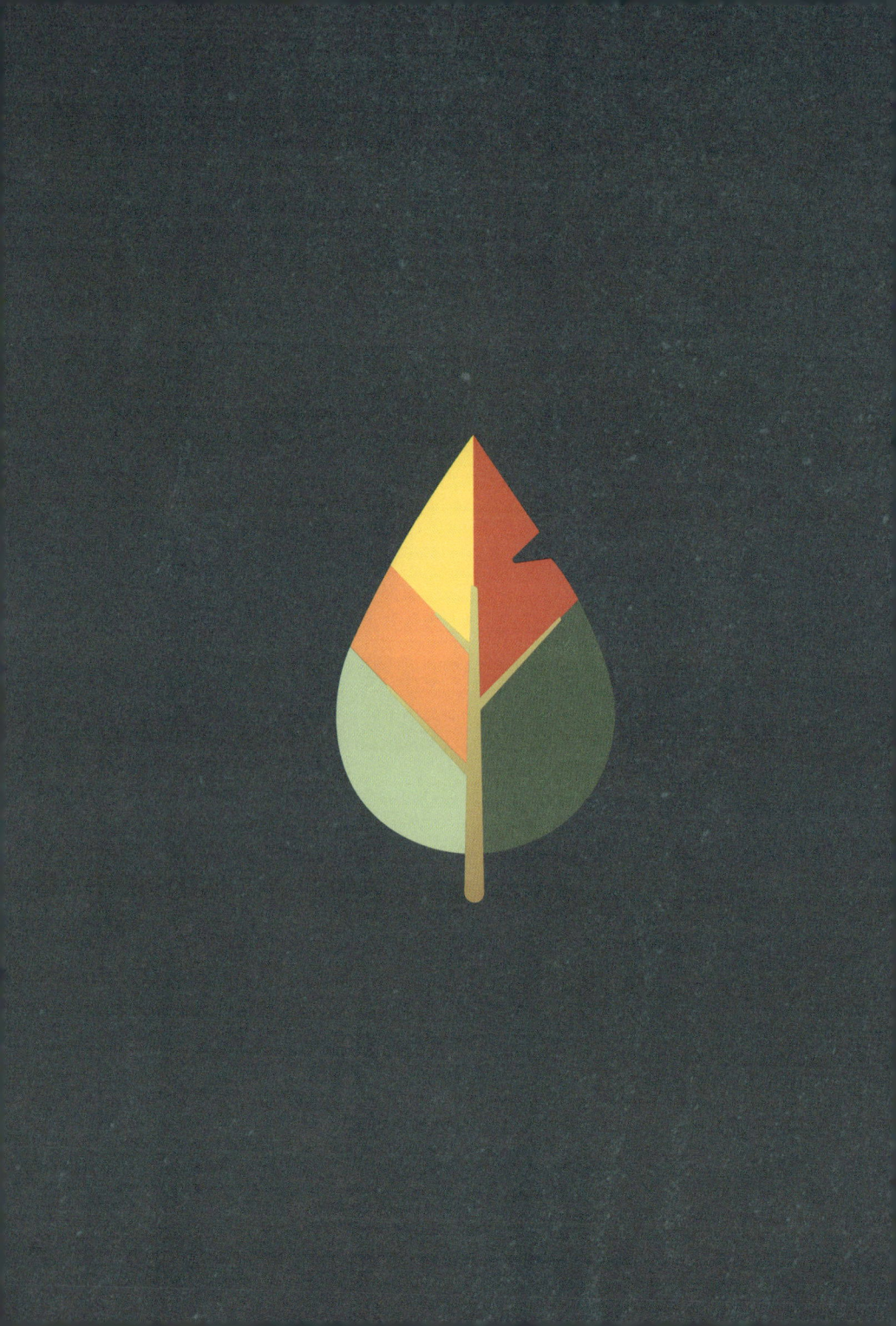

PART 5

WHOLENESS AT THE LORD'S TABLE

The Lord's Table. The Lord's Supper. Holy Communion. It goes by different names in different church traditions, but they all refer to taking a bit of bread and the fruit of the vine in holy remembrance of what Jesus accomplished for us on the Cross.

Given that physical healing was part of that atoning work Jesus carried out, this moment of remembrance is an ideal time to receive the healing that has already been graciously, abundantly supplied to us in Jesus.

Use the following devotions in the context of taking communion, alone or with others, as a vehicle for receiving healing.

HAPPY, HEALTHY, AND FREE

DAY
29

HEALING IN THE PASSOVER MEAL

At last, God freed all the Hebrews from their slavery and sent them away laden with the silver and gold of Egypt. And not even one was feeble on their way out!

PSALM 105:37

The 105th psalm is largely about the Israelites' exodus from Egypt. And this verse makes explicit something hinted at in the account in the book of Exodus. Namely that everyone among the hundreds of thousands, or more likely millions, of Israelites — including elderly people, all of whom had been subjected to brutal forced labor for many years — made the journey out of Egypt without a single one of them being physically unwell or weak.

The reason for this miracle is also there in the Exodus account. The night before their departure, God instructed them to prepare a special meal, the centerpiece of which was to be a perfect, unblemished sacrificial lamb.

As we saw in a previous devotion, the presence of the blood of that lamb on a household's doorpost caused the Destroyer to "pass over" the home. But it seems that meal had additional effects. It imparted miraculous, supernatural healing.

The new covenant parallel of that Passover meal is communion — the "meal" at which we remember that the ultimate and final Passover Lamb was sacrificed and bore all the consequences of our slavery to sin, setting us free.

YOUR WHOLENESS BLESSING

May you, having partaken of Jesus the Lamb, having had His blood sprinkled on the doorposts of your life, walk forward into freedom, whole and sound in every way.

THE BLOOD OF THAT LAMB ON A HOUSEHOLD'S DOORPOST CAUSED THE DESTROYER TO "PASS OVER" THE HOME.

HAPPY, HEALTHY, AND FREE

DAY
30

HIS BODY, BROKEN FOR YOU

I have handed down to you what came to me by direct revelation from the Lord himself. The same night in which he was handed over, he took bread and gave thanks. Then he distributed it to the disciples and said, "Take it and eat your fill. It is my body, which is given for you. Do this to remember me."

1 CORINTHIANS 11:23–24

Matthew's and Luke's accounts of what we commonly call "the Last Supper" contain one detail Paul doesn't provide here. Namely that Jesus *broke* the bread before passing it out to His disciples (Matthew 26:26). This is not a surprising detail. Everyone had to break up a loaf or sheet of bread before eating it in that day. The saying "It's the greatest invention since sliced bread" exists for a reason.

So, Jesus snapped the cracker-like pieces of unleavened bread in half, and then those halves into ever-smaller bits. Over and over again, the attentive disciples heard that distinctive crack of the bread being broken. And then He said four words in Matthew 26:26 that would roll down through the ages like thunder and ring in our ears now:

"This is my body."

"Take it," He said. Take it into yourself. Fill yourself up with Me. This body is about to be broken . . . for you. He broke the bread. Then hours later, He laid down His life on the Cross so His sinless body might be broken.

Yes, He was broken so that we could be whole — not just spiritually and emotionally, but physically too. Wholly whole.

YOUR WHOLENESS BLESSING

May you remember the awful price Jesus paid to restore you to your heavenly Father. His body was broken so that you might be utterly, fully, completely . . . whole.

HE WAS BROKEN SO THAT WE COULD BE WHOLE — NOT JUST SPIRITUALLY AND EMOTIONALLY, BUT PHYSICALLY TOO.

HAPPY, HEALTHY, AND FREE

DAY
31

REDEEMED BY HIS BLOOD

*Since we are now joined to Christ, we have been given **the treasures of redemption by his blood— the total cancellation of our sins**—all because of the cascading riches of his grace.*

EPHESIANS 1:7 (EMPHASIS ADDED)

Sickness and death entered the world when sin entered the world. For a loving God who longed to restore everything in creation that had been broken, twisted, and ravaged by sin, there could be no solution to sickness without first providing a solution to sin.

Scores of New Testament scriptures make it clear that the spotless, guiltless blood of a sinless Jesus was that solution.

- Colossians 1:20 declares that Jesus' blood brought about the reconciliation of all things, both in heaven and on earth.

- Romans 5:9 reveals that Jesus has justified us by His blood — meaning it makes us as if we had never sinned.

- Ephesians 1:7 shows us that the blood provides both redemption and forgiveness of our sins.

- First John 1:7 says the blood of *Christ cleanses us from all sin.*

- Hebrews 10:19 (NASB) says we now have *confidence to enter the holy place* — that is the very presence of God Himself — *by the blood of Jesus.*

- And two verses later, in Hebrews 10:22 (ESV), we learn that the blood results in us being free to run right into God's presence with *a true heart in full assurance of faith, with our hearts sprinkled clean from an evil conscience.*

Perhaps you're beginning to understand why Jesus, at what we commonly call "the Last Supper," held up a cup of wine and told His disciples, *"For this is the blood that seals the new covenant. It will be poured out for many for the complete forgiveness of sins"* (Matthew 26:28).

Wonder no longer whether or not you qualify for healing. Having been cleansed, redeemed, and made righteous by Jesus' blood, you qualify.

JESUS HAS JUSTIFIED US BY HIS BLOOD — MEANING IT MAKES US AS IF WE HAD NEVER SINNED.

YOUR WHOLENESS BLESSING

May you, with open arms, and a heart full of faith and gratitude, receive *the treasures of redemption* made possible by His blood. And know deep in your soul that among those treasures lies an extraordinary gem — healing for all of you!

HAVE YOU BEEN TO THE CROSS?

It's possible that this book did not hold much meaning or power for you because you've never appropriated Jesus' extraordinary sacrifice for your life. You do that by simply receiving the Father's free gift of salvation and eternal life, made possible through Jesus' sacrifice.

Jesus didn't just die for you. He died as you. He died on the Cross in your place. In His death, He took on all the bad you deserve, so you could receive all the good and blessing and life He deserved. Once you make the choice to receive that gift, nothing will ever be the same for you again.

ARE YOU READY TO RECEIVE THE FREE AND LIMITLESS GIFT OF SALVATION THROUGH JESUS CHRIST? IF SO, PRAY THIS PRAYER:

> *Father in heaven, I recognize that I can't reach You or heaven on my own. I have nothing to offer. Nothing to give. So I come to the Cross of Jesus now to receive Your free, gracious gift of forgiveness, cleansing, and eternal life.*
>
> *Right now, I take my guilt, my shame, my brokenness and lay it upon Jesus' Cross. I gratefully receive this amazing gift with gratitude and joy. Thank You!*

Did you pray that prayer? Here's good news. Romans 10:13 says: *"Everyone who calls on the Lord's name will experience new life"* (TPT).

Congratulations!

BREAKFAST FOR SEVEN

... So they [the disciples] went out and fished through the night, but caught nothing. ... Jesus shouted to them, "Throw your net over the starboard side, and you'll catch some!" And so they did as he said, and they caught so many fish they couldn't even pull in the net! Then the disciple whom Jesus loved said to Peter, "It's the Lord!" When Peter heard him say that, he quickly wrapped his outer garment around him, and because he was athletic, he dove right into the lake to go to Jesus! The other disciples then brought the boat to shore, dragging their catch of fish. They weren't far from land, only about a hundred meters. And when they got to shore, they noticed a charcoal fire with some roasted fish and bread. Then Jesus said, "Bring some of the fish you just caught." So Peter waded into the water and helped pull the net to shore. It was full of many large fish, exactly one hundred and fifty-three, but even with so many fish, the net was not torn. "Come, let's have some breakfast," Jesus said to them. And not one of the disciples needed to ask who it was, because every one of them knew it was the Lord. (John 21:3, 6–12, TPT)

Just after Jesus told seven of His disciples to cast their nets out the other side of the boat for a historical catch, He brought them ashore, sat down with them, encouraged them, and made them breakfast. At Breakfast for Seven, we believe it's time for you to cast your net out the other side.

breakfastforseven.com